Legends Folklore of Dorset

by Robert Hesketh

Inspiring Place Publishing
2 Down Lodge Close
Alderholt
Fordingbridge
SP6 3JA

ISBN 978-0-9928073-0-6
©Robert Hesketh 2013
All rights reserved
Contains Ordnance Survey data © Crown copyright and database right (2011)

Contents

Page

3	Introduction
4,5	Map of Locations
6	St Wite at Whitchurch Canonicorum (1)
7	Lyme Regis and Fossils (2)
8	Haunted Lyme Regis (2)
9	Bridport (3)
10	Powerstock (4) and Eggardon Hill (5)
11	Abbotsbury (6)
12	Weymouth (7)
13	Portland (8)
14	Cerne Abbas (9)
15	Athelhampton (10)
17	Tolpuddle (11)
18	Botany Bay Inn and the Red Post (12)
19	Clouds Hill (13)
20	Corfe Castle and King Edward the Martyr (14)
22	Smuggling and Isaac Gulliver (15)
24	Lulworth Cove (16) and Durdle Door (17)
25	Worbarrow Bay (18) and Wimborne Minster (19)
26	Badbury Rings (20)
27	Knowlton Church and prehistoric circle (21)
28	Corfe Mullen, the Coventry Arms (22)
29	The True Lovers Knot, Tarrant Keynston (23) and Christchurch Priory (24)
30	Christchurch, Mrs Perkins's Mausoleum (25)
31	The Cross in Hand, Batcombe Hill (26)
32	Pack Monday Fair, Sherborne (27)
33	Sherborne's Castles (28)
35	Shaftesbury Abbey (29)
36	Skimmington Ride at Montacute House (30)
37	Thornford Church Tithe Table (31)
38, 39	Calendar of Events
40	Bibliography, Further Reading and Tourist Information Centres

Introduction

Each major strata of Dorset's varied history has added to its rich heritage of legends, customs and folklore. Delving into these fascinating subjects, this guide will provide interesting and practical information to help you discover the sites around this beautiful county. There's a great deal to explore. Before science held sway, folklore explained the natural world, including the marvellous but perplexing fossils of the Jurassic Coast. Mingled with belief in witchcraft, folklore had dark aspects too, as the mummified cat at Corfe Mullen shows.

Imagination takes root where the past is but dimly known and understood, and legends of ghostly armies, gods and demons flowered in the fertile soil of Dorset's many prehistoric sites. Several, including the Cerne Abbas Giant, are said to have strange powers.

Legend surrounds the suspicious murder of St Edward the Martyr at Corfe Castle in 978 and the burning of Christchurch in 1113. It grows too around better recorded events in later centuries, including the death of T.E. Lawrence at Clouds Hill in 1935. His ghost is one of many said to haunt the county.

Although some customs have faded into disuse, others are alive and well. They include many May Day celebrations around the county, Sherborne's Pack Monday Fair and the Tolpuddle Festival. All provide a vibrant connection to Dorset's long history.

"Old" Sherborne Castle.

The Cobb at Lyme Regis.

Map of Locations

Directions and grid references are given for locations that are not obvious or detailed in the text.

The Dorset Flag.

1. St Wite at Whitchurch Canonicorum

Whitchurch Canonicorum's impressive church is an ideal starting point to explore the legends, customs and folklore of Dorset. It is dedicated to St Wite (also known as St Candida) and contains her shrine, within which is a leaden casket inscribed "Hic requesct relique Sce Wite" (Here rest the remains of St Wite). The casket contains the bones of a woman of about forty. These are thought to be the only ancient relics in England apart from those of St Edward the Confessor in Westminster Abbey to survive the Reformation.

It is not known for certain who St Wite was. According to local tradition, she was a Saxon holy woman killed by the Danes when they raided Charmouth in the ninth century. The medieval church venerated her as a martyr and pilgrims came to Whitchurch to seek her aid and healing. Pilgrims put their diseased limbs in oval openings in the base of the shrine or inserted handkerchiefs there, which they took away to heal the sick.

Reputed to heal diseased eyes, St Wite's Well has been known since the seventeenth century and lies 2km (1 ½ miles) south of Whitchurch Canonicorum. It was said St Wite lived nearby in prayer and contemplation. "St Candida's Eyes" is the local name for the wild periwinkles that grow on nearby Stonebarrow Hill.

Known as St Wite's Cross or the Dorset Cross, the county flag (page 5) was officially recognized in 2008. Similar in design to the Cornish St Piran's flag and St Petroc's, the flag of Devon, its gold background is associated with the golden dragon of Wessex and the Dorsetshire Regiment.

Whitchurch Canonicorum SY3979550, signed north from A35. St Wite's Well, SY399938, signed on footpath from minor lane just south of Morcombelake and the A35.

Above: The saint's shrine in the church.
Top right: St Wite's statue on the tower of St Candida's Church.

2. Lyme Regis and Fossils

The Jurassic rocks of Lyme Regis and neighbouring Charmouth are internationally famous for their fossils and have drawn the attention of scientists since the early nineteenth century, when Lyme Regis fossil hunter Mary Anning (1799-1847) found or pointed the way towards nearly every important palaeontological specimen. Thanks in no small measure to her dedicated collecting, Dorset holds a special place in the development of science and a rational understanding of the earth's age, origins and development.

Before fossilization and evolution were understood, fossils were explained through a rich assortment of folk tales and myths, reflected in their popular names. Among the best known are "snakestones", otherwise ammonites (left), extinct sea dwelling cephalopod molluscs. Low tide reveals a fascinating array of ammonites in the limestone fossil pavement of Monmouth Beach, west of the Cobb. Very numerous, they vary considerably in size and shape.

Snakestones were said to be coiled snakes, conger eels or monstrous sea serpents that had lost their heads and been turned to stone. "If you break them you find within stony serpents, wreathed up in circles, but eternally without heads," according to William Camden's *Britannia* (1586). By association, snakestones were carried as protection against snake bite in the same way that adder fat was used in Dorset to cure the effects of snake bite.

"Thunderbolts" or "Thunder Bullets" are the names given in Dorset to the slender bullet shaped fossils said to have been thrown down from the heavens during thunderstorms. Very common on the beaches of Lyme and Charmouth, they are belemnites, fossilized parts of a cuttlefish that, like ammonites, died out at the end of the Cretaceous Period.

Above: The "ammonite pavement" on Monmouth Beach, Lyme Regis, only exposed at low tide.

"Devil's toenails" is the popular name for the gnarled, curved fossilized shells of Gryphaea, an extinct oyster. These fossils are also common around Lyme as are "Fairy Loaves", small heart shaped fossilized shells of an ancient sea urchin. It was believed they were baked by fairies and imbued with magic. Fairy Loaves ensured a house would never be without bread, whilst milk kept by them would not sour.

*Fossil hunting is very rewarding at Lyme Regis and Charmouth, but please visit at low tide, stay well clear of the notoriously unstable cliffs and beware of slippery rocks and the returning tide. For the uninitiated, several fossil hunting expeditions are organized by experienced collectors.

Contact Lyme Regis TIC 01297 442138; Lyme Regis Museum (excellent fossil collection) 01297 443370 or Charmouth Heritage Coast Centre 01297 560772 (another good fossil collection).

Haunted Lyme Regis

Famous for fossils, Lyme Regis also has its place in English national history as the landing place of James, Duke of Monmouth in 1685. Monmouth was an illegitimate son of Charles II and his ill-considered plan to wrest the crown from his uncle, James II, led to ignominious defeat at the Battle of Sedgemoor. Many Dorset men had supported Monmouth, who posed as the Protestant champion against the radically Catholic James II. Many were condemned to death by the notorious Judge Jeffreys. Twelve were hanged on Monmouth Beach.

Whilst the ghostly figure of Monmouth mounted on a white horse has been reported in the harbour area, Jeffreys' ghost; replete with robes, wig and carrying a bloody bone, is said to haunt the Great House (Chatham House) in Broad Street, where he stayed. Another haunted place in Broad Street is the Royal Lion Hotel. Facing a former gallows site, it is troubled by disembodied footsteps and misty figures.

Higher up Broad Street is the Volunteer Inn. Here, a guest reportedly saw three men in seventeenth century musketeer uniforms drinking from tankards at the bar. Possibly, they were spirits from the English Civil War, when Parliamentarian forces withstood an eight week long siege by Prince Maurice in 1644.

Another Lyme inn with a curious tale is the Pilot Boat Inn, Bridge Street. After H.M.S. Formidable was torpedoed in 1915, survivors and dead crewmen were brought to the Pilot Boat. One sailor taken for dead was brought back to consciousness when Lassie, the landlord's dog, licked his face. She bore the same name as the canine heroine of Elizabeth Gaskell's 1859 story *The Half Brothers*, but antedated Eric Knight's 1940 novel *Lassie Come Home*, which was filmed in 1943.

Right: The Volunteer Inn.

3. Bridport

Bridport is one of several Dorset communities that continue the ancient traditions of May Day (see events calendar page 38). Maypole dancing, crowning the May Queen, country dancing, stalls and crafts are usual.

The town's rope making industry gave it a sinister reputation - hangmen's ropes were known as "Bridport Daggers". Flax and hemp grew well in the area and were spun by hand in "rope walks" along the town's old streets.

A memorial stone (below right) in Lee Lane on the town's eastern outskirts at the junction with the A35 marks King Charles II's escape route on 23 September, 1651. Charles had been forced to flee after defeat at the Battle of Worcester. He had several narrow escapes from his enemies, moving secretly from one hiding place to another around England, as described by Arthur Bryant in his biography.

Charles's most celebrated escape was shortly after the battle, when he hid from Parliamentarian troopers in an oak tree near Boscobel House, Shropshire, an event that has become part of English folklore. Remembered in Oak Apple Day on 29th May, the anniversary of Charles's Restoration to the throne in 1660, it is depicted on many English inn signs, including the Royal Oak at Cerne Abbas (page 14).

Hoping to find a ship to take him to France, Charles made towards the south coast. Disguised as a plain countryman, he posed as the attendant of Jane Lane, the daughter of his faithful follower, Colonel Lane. After a week riding pillion with Jane, Charles found shelter at Trent House near Sherborne, home of Colonel Francis Wyndham, another Royalist officer.

Always fortunate with the ladies, Charles again rode pillion, this time with Wyndham's niece, Juliana Coningsby. Reaching Charmouth, they posed as a runaway couple and put up at the Queen's Arms. Charles's friend, Wilmot, tried to negotiate with a Captain Limbry to give him safe passage to France. This attempt was foiled (according to Limbry) by Mrs. Limbry who locked her husband in their bedroom for his own safety!

Again in danger of his life with a £1,000 reward on his head, Charles made for Bridport with Juliana and put up at the George. Realizing Parliamentarian troopers were on their trail, they left hastily and rode a short distance along the London road (today's A35), before turning up Lee Lane. In doing so they lost their pursuers and made for safety at Broadwindsor, where they stayed at the village inn.

Here, Charles had a narrow escape from a different party of soldiers, who were distracted when one of the women travelling with them went into labour. Charles returned to Trent House once more. Whilst hiding there he was amused to hear the church bells of Trent pealing and a crowd of villagers dancing round a bonfire in celebration of his supposed death and capture.

Looking again to escape England, Charles rode east. After further adventures (described in some detail by Bryant) he eventually took ship from Shoreham in Sussex to safety and exile in France.

4. Powerstock

In the churchyard of St Mary's, Powerstock is a thirteenth century dole table (right), a very rare survival. Doles of bread were distributed to the poor from it. (See page 37 for Thornford Church's tithe table). SY517963.

5. Eggardon Hill

Eggardon Hill's Iron Age fort is a superb viewpoint at 252m (831ft) above sea level. It covers some 8ha (20 acres) and is defended by three massive ramparts. Looking out from these on a fine day gives a sense of tranquil timelessness...and yet Eggardon is said to be haunted. Diana, goddess of the moon and hunting joins here with demons, witches and fairies collecting the souls of the dead. Dogs and horses have been reported terrified on visiting Eggardon for no apparent reason, while motorists passing by on the road to Powerstock have had their car engines suddenly die and their watches stop for a time.

Eggardon Hill, SE of Powerstock, SY542947

Eggardon Hill

6. Abbotsbury

Abbotsbury celebrates the coming of May with Garland Day, traditionally held on May 13. Two garlands of flowers are paraded through the village. Formerly, they were then cast into the sea, but these days they are placed beside the war memorial in the churchyard.

St Catherine's Chapel, just south of Abbotsbury, was built in the fourteenth century as a place of pilgrimage and retreat. According to Udal (*Dorsetshire Folk –Lore*) unmarried women would visit the chapel and, placing their hands and knees in the "wishing holes" in the south doorway, invoke the aid of St Catherine to find them husbands by chanting this prayer:

"A husband, St Catherine;
A handsome one, St Catherine;
A rich one, St Catherine;
A nice one, St Catherine;
And soon, St Catherine."

It is also said that women wishing to find husbands should visit St Augustine's Well at Cerne Abbas (page 14), especially on May Day, Midsummer's Day or St Catherine's Day, 25th November. The woman should immerse herself in the water and drink it.

St Catherine's Chapel, English Heritage, open any reasonable time. Follow path from the village off B3157. Path leads off signposted lane to Swannery. SY573848.

Keeping swans is an ancient tradition at Abbotsbury, where the Swannery on the western tip of Fleet Lagoon has up to 600 birds and is the oldest managed swan population in the world. First recorded in 1393, it was

established by the Benedictine monks of Abbotsbury. After Henry VIII's Dissolution of the Monasteries, ownership passed to the Fox-Strangways family, the Earls of Ilchester, who own Abbotsbury village and estate.

Signposted from Abbotsbury, it is open to the public (01305 871858).
Above right: St Catherine's Chapel.

The lovely Georgian sea front at Weymouth.

7. Weymouth

Statue of King George III, Weymouth.

Since the late eighteenth century Dorset has been associated with sea bathing and seaside holidays. Weymouth developed early as a resort and gained a massive boost in 1789 when King George III stayed there in Gloucester Lodge, accompanied by Queen Charlotte and the Princesses Charlotte, Augusta and Elizabeth – though the scapegrace Prince of Wales was conspicuously absent.

His Majesty walked on the promenade, where he endured a long winded address from the Mayor. He was greeted with general acclamation as he stepped forth from his bathing machine, which was decorated with the British flag and the King's Royal Coat of Arms. As he emerged from the briny a band struck up with "God save great George our King."

Possibly to escape these embarrassments, George spent much of his time sailing off Portland – again, royal patronage helped promote both the place and the sport: Portland is a great sailing centre today. However, George's female companions cared little for sailing and preferred the family drives to Lulworth, Milton Abbey and Sherborne. They patronized pony racing on Weymouth Sands; visited the theatre in Augusta Place and worshipped regularly at the parish church.

All in all, George's first Weymouth holiday was a great success and lasted ten weeks. The Royal Family became regular visitors to Weymouth between 1791 and 1805, adding prestige and popularity not only to Dorset but the English seaside as an institution at a time when patriotism ran high and foreign holidays were all but impossible because of the wars with France.

8. The Isle of Portland

"Carved by Time out of a single stone" was how Thomas Hardy described Portland. He called it the "Isle of Slingers" allegedly because the fiercely independent locals hurled rocks at strangers. However, the Romans may have used this nickname because Chesil Beach provided millions of pebbles as ammunition for the British slingers.

Rabbits are seen as extremely bad luck on Portland, probably because their burrowing can cause landslips. Men working in the island's many quarries are said to have downed tools if a rabbit was seen and gone home until their safety was assured, whilst fishermen would refuse to go to sea if "rabbit" was mentioned. Rabbits are as unspeakable among conservative Portlanders as Macbeth is among actors, being referred to as "underground mutton" or "furry things". Accordingly, poster advertisements on Portland in 2005 for the Wallace and Grommit film "Curse of the Were Rabbit" were replaced with the inoffensive phrase "something bunny is going on".

A fabulous bird was seen off Portland in November 1547 "coming out of the sea with a great crest on its head, a great red beard, and legs half a yard long", according to a report quoted in Udal from the sixteenth century chronicler, Holinshead. "He stood on the water and crowed three times, and every time turned himself about and beckoned with his head north south east and west. He was in colour like a pheasant and when he crowed he vanished."

What might this signify? One possibility, given England's often belligerent and stormy relations with her near neighbours, is France. The cock has been an unofficial symbol of France since Roman times, possibly being a play on words: gallus (Latin for cockerel) and Gallus (Gallic). The late Rodney Legg in his *Mysterious Dorset* speculated it might have been the figure head of a wrecked ship.

Old quarry workings near Portland Bill.

9. Cerne Abbas

Cerne's most celebrated figure - the Giant - is unmistakable. Cut into the chalk of Trendle Hill he is 180ft long, 167ft wide and brandishes a club 120ft long in his right hand. Both a triumphant and a phallic symbol, his age and origins have been much debated.

Although the earliest record of the Giant only dates from 1742, it is probable he is Romano-British, perhaps a British Hercules, a cult figure symbolizing strength and fertility, though it is possible his pagan roots are even older. Certainly, he resembles Roman coins, statuettes and Castor ware representing Hercules. He may well date from the time of Commodus (AD180-93). After defeating the Scots in 187, Commodus declared himself Hercules incarnate and added Hercules Romanus to his titles.

Whatever his age, the Giant is the focus of customs and legends. Reputedly, the original Giant terrorized the village before he was killed and beheaded on the hill where his outline was traced in the chalk as a terrible reminder of his awesome size. He is rumoured to have magical powers to bring fertility to childless couples, especially if they lie on him together on May Day, an event he has long been associated with.

Traditionally, Morris Men dance above the Giant and then in the village square during the village's May Day celebrations, which commence at dawn. A maypole was erected on the Giant too, until suppressed by Puritans in 1635. They built a town ladder with the timber.

Cerne's high minded Puritans anticipated Parliament which, in tacit acknowledgement of the maypole's pagan associations with fertility, banned them all in 1644. Charles II's Restoration in 1660 brought a change of attitude and maypoles were reinstated in many Dorset communities, featuring in several modern May Day celebrations (page 38).

Follow road signs to Cerne Abbas Giant, ST016666.

Left: The Cerne Giant.
Above: The Silver Well.
Facing page: The Abbot's Porch, part of the old Cerne Abbey.

Cerne Abbas grew around its Benedictine monastery, founded in 987, but the well in Cerne Abbas churchyard is said to be even older. Like Moses striking the rock with his staff, St Augustine of Canterbury struck his staff in the ground causing a spring to issue forth when he visited the area during his great mission to convert the English between 596 and 605.

A second legend attached to the well is that St Edwold had his hermitage there in the seventh century. Following a vision, he came to Cerne Abbas, where he gave silver pennies to shepherds who showed him the well and gave him food and water. It is said to be beneficial to dip new born babies in the well as the first rays of the sun touch the water. Certainly, it is a place of charm and tranquility.

Follow Abbey Street to its end, where the remains of the Abbey, including the Abbot's Porch and guest house, are signed. Turn right into the churchyard and follow the wall for 100m. ST666012.

10. Athelhampton

Athelhampton is said to be one of the most haunted houses in England. This beautiful manor was built around 1485 by Sir William Martyn, who received a licence from the newly crowned Henry VII, victor of Bosworth, to enclose 160 acres of deer park and fortify his home. The crenellated parts of Athelhampton are thus the oldest, whilst the West Wing was added in the early sixteenth century and the whole was restored with the formal gardens we see today in the late nineteenth century.

Visitors first enter the Great Hall, where a guest was disturbed by the apparitions of two young men in seventeenth century garb fighting a duel. She demanded they stop, but they ignored her and fought on until one was cut across the arm. At this point, they left the room. When the lady asked the owner who they might be, he was as perplexed as she. It is thought the duellists might have been spirits from Civil War times, when Athelhampton supported the Royalist cause.

The Great Hall's oriel windows have fascinating sixteenth century heraldic stained glass, including images of an ape. This is ironic, as a pet ape haunts the priest hole in the neighbouring Great Chamber. The unfortunate animal was accidentally imprisoned and died of thirst and hunger in this secret passage, which was intended to hide Catholic clergy during times of religious persecution. Though never seen, its ghostly scratching can be heard from behind the panels as it tries desperately to escape.

A cat haunts the Great Stairway, where the soft padding of its paws has been heard. The figure of a priest dressed in black was seen by one of the housemaids by the bathroom, whilst the sound of tapping from the wine cellar is ascribed to a ghostly cooper. Some visitors to the King's Room have reported feeling inexplicably cold and intensely uncomfortable, phenomena often associated with ghosts. Haunted too is the State Bedroom: a grey lady sits on the bed, but she will obligingly disappear if asked to do so.

Athelhampton House DT2 7LG 01305 848363 signed from Tolpuddle/Puddletown road at SY772945.

Above: The water garden at Athelhampton.
Left: The West Wing of the great house, completed in the 15th century.
Facing page: The Martyrs' Shelter at Tolpuddle.

11. Tolpuddle

Tolpuddle has a central place in labour and trade union history. National attention was focussed on this quiet village between Dorchester and Bere Regis in 1834 when six Tolpuddle farm labourers were sentenced to transportation, nominally for swearing an illegal oath, in reality for forming a trade union and thus challenging the authority of landowners and magistrates, the rural Establishment.

The story of the six "Tolpuddle Martyrs" as they became known was set against a background of severe and worsening rural poverty, exacerbated by wage cuts. This had already provoked violent discontent across southern England during 1830-31. It was led by the mythical "Captain Swing", under whose name threats to burn ricks and break machinery were issued unless wages and conditions were improved. Responding with savage punishments to violations of property, the authorities sentenced some 500 people to transportation and 200 to death – of whom 19 were hanged. In Dorchester, a special commission tried 62 prisoners following the Captain Swing disturbances and sentenced 13 to transportation for life.

Since the repeal of the Combination Acts in 1824, forming a trade union or friendly society was legal, and the infant trade union movement  was gaining in numbers and strength. However, collective organizations were viewed with deep suspicion by many, not least James Frampton. A Dorset landowner and Colonel of the Dorset Yeomanry, Frampton had passed heavy sentences on Captain Swing rioters in his capacity as a chief magistrate in 1831.

Three years later, the six Tolpuddle labourers were brought to trial at Dorchester Assizes through the machinations of Frampton in collusion with Home Secretary, Lord Melbourne under two earlier acts outlawing secret oaths, which they had unwisely made.

News of the Tolpuddle men's sentences – seven years transportation - provoked uproar in the national press, mass demonstrations and petitions to the Prime Minister and the King. Nonetheless, the six were transported and served as slave labour in Australia under brutal conditions. Squire Frampton ensured their families in Tolpuddle were denied parish relief. They survived on funds raised by the London Dorchester Committee.

Largely due to the work of radicals, especially Thomas Wakeley MP and the new Home Secretary, Lord John Russell, the Tolpuddle Martyrs were eventually granted a full pardon by King William IV after serving three years. Their remarkable story and the harsh realities of nineteenth century life in rural Dorset are told in vivid detail in the Tolpuddle Martyrs Museum, from where visitors can follow the "Tolpuddle Martyrs Trail" around the village.

This includes the grave of James Hammett (one of the six) in the churchyard and the Martyrs' Tree under which the friendly society they formed met. It continues past the Martyrs' Inn to Thomas Standfield's Cottage, where the six took the oath that resulted in their conviction and on by the Methodist Chapel, successor to the one their leader, George Loveless, preached in. The trail ends by the Memorial Arch. This commemorates their history, which continues to inspire the trade union movement.

Keeping the story of the Tolpuddle Martyrs alive, the annual three day long Tolpuddle Festival (above) includes speeches, live music and a variety of stalls and entertainments. It culminates in a lively procession through the village in which trade unionists from all over Britain, including a strong Dorset contingent, march with flags, banners, musicians and dancers.

Tolpuddle Martyrs Museum DT2 7EH, 01305 848237. Signed from A35, SY795945.

12. Botany Bay Inn and the Red Post

The Botany Bay Inn is on the south side of the A31, one mile east of the Red Post (SY883971) at SY898973. Its name has a curious history. Prisoners such as the Tolpuddle Martyrs (page 17) sentenced to transportation in the Botany Bay penal settlements in Australia were sent under escort from Dorchester Jail to

Portsmouth, where they embarked. The Red Post directed the escorts, who were often illiterate, to the first staging post of this sad journey, Botany Bay Barn. There the prisoners were shackled for the night before continuing east. The ruins of the barn lie half a mile south of Red Post along the lane.

Dorset has several other red posts. One is located near Evershot (above right) at ST550039, another north of Sherborne at ST640198. Another souvenir of transportation is a plaque on the parapet on the sixteenth century bridge near Sturminster Marshall where the road crosses the river Stour at White Mill (ST957007) (page 28). It dates from the 1820s and reads:

"Any person willfully injuring any part of this county bridge will be guilty of a felony and upon conviction be liable to be transported for life. By the court. T Fooks."

13. Clouds Hill

Bearing the inscription "Don't Worry" in Greek over the lintel, Clouds Hill was the retreat of T.E. Lawrence, the legendary and enigmatic "Lawrence of Arabia". His strong, complex and often contradictory personality is deeply impressed upon this tiny brick and tile labourer's cottage, which he restored, altered and furnished.

Clouds Hill gave Lawrence the peace and solitude he needed to write, most famously to revise *Seven Pillars of Wisdom*, his autobiographical account of the Arab Revolt of 1916-18, which he did much to inspire and shape. In contrast to the stalemate and carnage of the Western Front, the fast moving desert campaign brought victory at a relatively low cost in blood and treasure. It made Colonel Lawrence a national hero.

Lawrence's cottage.

However, this essentially shy and sensitive man was overwhelmed by the attention focussed upon him. Traumatized by his wartime experiences and angered by the shabby treatment of his Arab allies and their cause at the Versailles Peace Conference, he disappeared from public life and enlisted in the ranks of first the R.A.F. and then the Tank Corps under assumed names.

Although he found the simplicity of service life congenial and its austerity familiar after fighting in Arabia, Lawrence needed Clouds Hill to express the fullness of his talents. Conveniently close to Bovington Camp where he served, Clouds Hill was the place for him to dream, to write, or to listen to Beethoven and Mozart on his treasured gramophone. Lawrence applied his practical talents to the cottage, adding a water supply, a bath, a boiler and a bathing pool. He damp proofed the ceilings with aluminium foil and designed much of the furniture and many of the fittings. Bookshelves reach from floor to ceiling. Many of the copies were inscribed by leading literary figures, some of whom visited Clouds Hill, including Thomas Hardy, G.B. Shaw and E.M. Forster.

His twelve year term of service completed, Lawrence retired to Clouds Hill in 1935. *Seven Pillars of Wisdom*, initially written for a small subscription audience, had sold extraordinarily well and Lawrence's future appeared to open with rich new possibilities. They were not to be fulfilled. Only a few weeks later, he died from injuries he sustained after losing control of his Brough Superior motorcycle near Clouds Hill. A memorial stone marks the scene of this tragedy, where the roar of Lawrence's Brough is said to haunt the road before dawn.

Lawrence's grave is at Moreton cemetery. His funeral was a tribute to the breadth of his influence and drew many mourners. Among literary and political figures present were Winston and Clementine Churchill, who had known Lawrence well. The funeral also drew the national press and, perhaps inevitably, a series of conspiracy theories about his sudden death arose which persist to the present day. These centre on a mysterious black car that was reported at the scene of the accident, but never identified.

A century after the First World War and more than fifty years after David Lean's coup de cinema, Lawrence of Arabia, interest in T.E. Lawrence is as strong as ever. Much can be learned about this intriguing man from visiting Clouds Hill and Wareham's Town Museum, which has a special Lawrence collection. A life-size statue of Lawrence in Arab dress by Eric Kennington rests at St Martin's in Wareham, a remarkable Anglo-Saxon church with twelfth century frescoes.

Clouds Hill (National Trust) BH20 7NQ, SY824909. Contact 01929 405616.
Lawrence's memorial stone is 500m south of Clouds Hill on east side of road by parking area at SY826904.
Lawrence's grave: Moreton cemetery SY804892.
Wareham Town Museum, East Street, BH20 4NN. 01929 553448.
St Martin's church, North Street, Wareham BH20 4AG.

14. Corfe Castle and King Edward the Martyr

Occupying a strong defensive position, Corfe Castle (right) dominates the entrance to the Isle of Purbeck. The romantic hilltop ruin we see today is the work of Parliamentarian sappers, who slighted Corfe Castle with mines and gunpowder in 1646. They had good reason to destroy the castle's military power. Under the command of the redoubtable Lady Mary Bankes, Corfe Castle had withstood two Civil War sieges and was only taken after one of its Royalist defenders treacherously admitted enemy troopers.

Corfe's history stretches back beyond the building of its classic Norman keep (1105) and later medieval defensive additions. It was probably a fortified site long before 978, when King Edward the Martyr was murdered here. Stabbed and wounded, he fell from his horse, which bolted, dragging him along by a stirrup. Who was responsible for the grisly deed is uncertain, some historians lay the blame on his step-mother, Elfrida (also known as Aelfthryth), others the supporters of his half-brother, Ethelred.

Edward was the eldest son of King Edgar, but not his acknowledged heir. When Edgar died in 975, the crown was contested. Some supported Edward, some Ethelred, the son of Edgar and Elfrida. It was a situation ripe for intrigue, especially as Edward was only in his teens. He was also of a violent and unstable temperament, according to "The Life of Oswald", a contemporary account.

However, The Anglo-Saxon Chronicle gives a different view of young Edward: "978: In this year, King Edward was murdered in the evening at Corfe 'passage': he was buried at Wareham with no royal honours. No worse deed was ever done among the English than this was, since first they sought the land of Britain. Men murdered him, but God exalted him; in life he was an earthly king, but after death he is now a heavenly saint..."

As with many of the people and events in Anglo-Saxon England, the exact truth of both Edward's character and his death are open to speculation. Very possibly, the opposing pictures of an obnoxious youth and a martyred saint are both wrong.

Either way, Edward is the stuff of legend. So too is his apparently wicked step-mother, Elfrida. She ruled as regent after Edward's murder until Ethelred came of age in 984. However, she appears to have been a religious woman, or at least a wicked but penitent woman who turned to religion. Elfrida founded Wherwell Abbey, a Benedictine nunnery in Hampshire, in about 986. Later in life, she retired to Wherwell and died there around 1000.

Meanwhile, Edward was en route to becoming a martyr and a saint. Following his hasty burial at Wareham, he was disinterred. His body was said to be miraculously preserved, which was taken as a sign of sainthood. Edward was reburied at Shaftesbury and later enshrined at Shaftesbury Abbey (page 35). Miracles associated with him were reported; pilgrims came to Shaftesbury and a cult developed around his memory.

Regarded as sacred relics, his bones were hidden from Henry VIII's iconoclasts during the Dissolution of the Monasteries, when many such relics were destroyed. In 1931, the bones of a young man were discovered in Shaftesbury Abbey during archaeological excavations. It was later confirmed they belonged to someone who met his death as Edward did and radio carbon dated to around 900AD. Today, they are enshrined in the Orthodox Church of Saint Edward the Martyr in Brookwood, Surrey.

A large painting of Edward in the square of Corfe Castle is captioned "Edward the Martyr King of Wessex treacherously stabbed at Corfe's Gate in AD 978 by his stepmother Elfrida". Behind the square is St Edward's Church. Other churches dedicated to his memory are located in Cambridge and Goathurst, Somerset.

Corfe Castle (National Trust) BH20 5EZ, 01929 481294, SY959824.

15. Smuggling and Isaac Gulliver

With its long coastline, sandy beaches and secluded coves, Dorset was well suited to play a prominent role in smuggling. Good communications with major sources of contraband in the Channel Islands and northern France, plus long traditions of sailing, boatbuilding and fishing were further advantages enjoyed by Dorset smugglers, or "free traders" as they preferred to call themselves.

The popular image of smugglers as clever underdogs outmanoeuvring the dull-witted authorities to bring romance, adventure and such luxuries as brandy, tobacco and silk into the lives of poor people on subsistence wages at affordable prices is appealing. It is even partly true. However, the other half of the story is that smugglers often resorted to violence and intimidation, which was inevitable as they challenged the armed authority of the state.

Because smugglers operated in secret as far as possible, evidence about them comes largely from their opponents in the Revenue, the Coastguard and the courts. Not surprisingly, legends grew around the smugglers and their clandestine activities.

More is known of Isaac Gulliver (1745-1822) the "King of the Smugglers", than most of his colleagues, though mystery and intrigue surround many of his operations, especially his relationship with the

Left: Winspit on the Isle of Purbeck, a favourite drop off point for smugglers.
Top next page: The beach west of Durdle Door. Under the headland of Bat's Head sits a cave used by smugglers.

authorities. Gulliver controlled contraband on the Dorset coast at the height of the classic smuggling era. He is said to have had a gang of fifty men identifiable by their white wigs, who operated fifteen luggers bringing spirits, lace, silks and tea from the Continent. Britain's frequent wars with France were no bar, but rather a great bonus to
his trade. In the first place, the Navy and Army were frequently occupied with fighting the enemy rather than pursuing smugglers (whom they often colluded with anyway). Secondly, the wars appear to have opened large and lucrative opportunities for Gulliver.

A Custom House report from Poole in 1788 admitted Gulliver was "one of the greatest and most notorious smugglers in the West of England". However, the report continued: "In the year 1782 he took the benefit of his Majesty's proclamation for pardoning such offences and as we are informed dropped that branch of smuggling and afterwards confined himself chiefly to the wine trade."

On the face of it, the pardon and Gulliver's switch to legal trade seems remarkable. It was made possible by the Act of Oblivion of 1782, which permitted smugglers to redeem their crimes by finding men to serve in the armed forces, where they were desperately needed to fight the smugglers' chief trading partners – the French.

Established as a wine merchant in Teignmouth, Gulliver continued smuggling as before and may well have used his illegal trade with France to gather strategic information for the British government in return for immunity. The business community also colluded with Gulliver. William Fryer, a Wimborne banker, was his financier and later son-in-law.

Gulliver is said to have run one of his largest and most profitable contraband cargoes ashore near where Bournemouth Pier now stands in 1800. Evidently, he continued to prosper and died in 1822, leaving a very substantial estate of £60,000 and properties scattered across the West Country. He completed his elevation to respectability by being buried in Wimborne Minster.

Many Dorset places are associated with Gulliver. Favoured landing places for contraband included Hengistbury Head, the Bournemouth beaches, Winspit, Worbarrow Bay, Lulworth Cove and Osmington Mills. Further west, Portland with its ledges and quarries were convenient for landing and storing contraband, whilst the quarrymen provided a ready labour force. Durdle Door, Chesil Beach and the several beaches of Lyme Bay including Lyme Regis were well known to Gulliver and his associates.

Gulliver planted trees to act as a daymark for his smuggling vessels on Eggardon Hill (page 10). Kinson House, now subsumed in Bournemouth, was one of his many Dorset addresses. He is reputed to have used several places in Kinson to store contraband; including St Andrew's Church, where ledges on the tower were damaged as kegs of brandy were hauled up.

16. Lulworth Cove

A superb natural harbour, Lulworth Cove (below) was a landing place for contraband. It is also said to be haunted. During the Second World War, the area was strongly defended to prevent any enemy invasion, whilst the cove was sealed off and mined, with lookouts posted on the cliffs. The lookouts were astonished to see people dancing in the moonlight on Lulworth's beach. Suddenly, they vanished. The area was carefully searched and the defences checked, but the ghostly dancers reappeared some nights later.

Lulworth Cove SY823801.

17. Durdle Door

Ghosts have also been reported at nearby Durdle Door, apparitions of young girls dancing on the waves. This haunting appears to be quite unconnected with the tragic death of Lieutenant Thomas Edward Knight, a Chief Coastguard Officer. He was set upon by a smuggling gang in June 1832 and thrown off the cliff near Durdle Door.

Durdle Door SY808803.

Durdle Door at dusk.

18. Worbarrow Bay

By contrast, the ghost of a smuggler killed by Revenue men is said to haunt Worbarrow Bay just east of Lulworth Cove. He was pursued along the beach and trapped between the sheer chalk cliffs and the sea, where he was ruthlessly stoned to death. His screams can be heard mingling with the crashing waves and his hapless figure is seen struggling through the surf.

Worbarrow Bay SY870795, BH20 5DE. Access via Tyneham. Part of army ranges, open most weekends and school holidays - 01929 414819.

19. Wimborne Minster

Wimborne's minster church is essentially Norman with later additions. Its roots go back to the eighth century, when Cuthburga, sister of King Ina, founded a nunnery in Wimborne about 705. True to form, Danes destroyed this in the 1013, but Edward the Confessor revived Wimborne's religious life by creating a college of secular canons.
    There is much to discover in the minster, including three curious monuments to Time. On the outside of the tower is the early nineteenth century quarter jack, a British Redcoat dressed in the uniform of the day who strikes his bells with a hammer in each hand.

Left: Anthony Ettricke's tomb in Wimborne Minster. Top page 27: The Iron Age hillfort of Badbury Rings, one of the sites claimed as the scene of King Arthur's last battle. Bottom page 27: Knowlton Church.

Far older is the astronomical clock inside the tower. Although its case is Elizabethan, its workings are medieval, the first record of their repair dates from 1409. A stationary Earth is shown at the centre of the clock with the moon and sun revolving around it – a cosmology developed by the Greek astronomer Ptolemy in the second century AD. Despite proofs provided by the controversial and revolutionary work of Nikolaus Copernicus (1473-1543) that the Earth is a planet revolving around the Sun, Ptolemy's system long remained part of the Catholic Church's dogma – Galileo Galilei was placed under house arrest for life in 1633 for supporting it and the Church's prohibitions on Copernicus's writing were not finally dropped until 1835.

Look carefully at the tomb of Anthony Ettricke in the chancel and you will notice that the year of his death has been changed from 1693 to 1703. Ettricke was convinced he would die in 1693, when he would have achieved his Biblical span of three score years and ten. He had his colourful tomb duly prepared for his expected decease – and went on to live another ten years. Given his professional background, his judgment should have been more accurate: Ettricke was Recorder of the Borough of Poole and the magistrate who sent the Duke of Monmouth for trial in 1685. Ettricke is also remembered by a pub in Wimborne's West Borough called The Man in the Wall, which bears a plaque to him.

20. Badbury Rings

Badbury Rings, like Eggardon (page 10), is a haunted Iron Age hillfort. It is said to have been the site of the Battle of Badon, though Bathampton Down in Somerset and Bowden Hill in Linlithgow also claim that honour. However, there is general agreement that Badon was a British victory in the early sixth century which severely checked the Saxons' westward advance.

The legendary King Arthur killed at least one hundred and sixty men at the Battle of Badon. He and his spectral army are said to return to the scene of their triumph on Badbury Rings. Archaeology students camping on Badbury Rings in 1970 were so terrified when awoken one night by clashing swords, marching feet and the cries of men that they fled their tents. Similar manifestations continued for several years afterwards. A ghostly warrior with a hideously scarred face was also reported, as well as another warrior on horseback, a woman in a black dress and a menacing dwarf that peers at couples.

Signed parking area at ST960032 off B3082 Blandford/Wimborne road.

21. Knowlton Church and prehistoric circles

Built within a Neolithic ritual henge, a substantial site with four earthworks or rings, Knowlton's ruined twelfth to fifteenth century church symbolizes the transition from pagan to Christian worship. Indeed, the church, with its flint and stone banding so characteristic of Dorset's high chalk country, may well incorporate stones from the pre-Christian site. Churches were built on former pagan sites in many places across Europe, including Brentor near Tavistock in Devon, but Knowlton's history has other interesting layers. Knowlton Rings was used as a meeting place for the local Saxon Hundred when Knowlton was a thriving village with a well known annual fair. Like many English villages, Knowlton reached its zenith in the high Middle Ages and then declined with

Above: Whitemill Bridge at Sturminster Marshall, from which Knowlton Church's bell is said to have been thrown.

the catastrophic population loss caused by bubonic plague - though in Knowlton's case the plague struck in 1485, long after the most notorious outbreak of bubonic plague, the terrible Black Death, in 1348/49. The church continued in use until the eighteenth century and today Knowlton is no more than a hamlet.

According to a legend recounted by JS Udal, Knowlton's church bell was stolen. The thieves managed to take it only as far as White Mill Bridge (see also page 18) near Sturminster Marshall, where they threw it into the River Stour and fled their pursuers. All attempts to pull the bell from the river were frustrated as the ropes attached to it inexplicably broke. Evidence for the present whereabouts of the bell is lacking. Some sources claim it is still in the river, others that it ended up either in Shapwick's church or Sturminster Marshall's church.

English Heritage: Parking area on narrow lane off B3078 Wimborne/Cranborne road, SU023102.

22. Corfe Mullen, the Coventry Arms

The Coventry Arms is a fine old inn with flag floors and exposed beams. The cock on its sign is emblematic of the Coventry family, but more curious is the mummified cat in a glass case by the bar. It was discovered under the roof, where it was put some 500 years ago.

Cats feature prominently in folklore about witches and were said to be their familiars. It is probable the unfortunate cat was sealed into the roof whilst still alive to ward off evil spirits and witchcraft.

Mummified cats have been discovered in the wall spaces and roofs of several old houses in various locations, including the Nutshell Inn, Bury St Edmunds in Suffolk, where a cat hangs over the bar. Another mummified cat was discovered in a house in Pendle, Lancashire, a notorious centre for witchcraft. In 1612, nine women and two men from Pendle were tried for witchcraft at Lancaster Assizes and all but one was hanged.

Coventry Arms, on A31 near Corfe Mullen, SY975984, BH21 3RH.

23. The True Lovers Knot, Tarrant Keynston

There are several stories to explain the origin of this inn's very unusual and possibly unique name. One is that the son of an early landlord fell in love with the daughter of a Dorset noble. They conducted their romance in secret, but were discovered by a servant. The noble was furious and forbade his daughter to see the young man. Quite distraught, she hanged herself. Overcome with grief, her lover too took the same fatal course. This left the noble a childless widower and he also hanged himself – hence the True Lovers Knot has three loops. In an equally tragic explanation, the daughter of an early landlord was raped by three men. He took his revenge by hanging them with one rope tied in "a true lover's knot".

A third and more hopeful explanation is that the inn was named after the knots which secured the masts to sailing ships. Sailors would send miniature versions of these knots to their sweethearts. If they could untie the knot it was understood the romance would continue.

True Lovers Knot, DT11 9JG, on B3082 between Wimborne and Blandford, ST933047.

24. Christchurch Priory

Christchurch's magnificent twelfth century priory church was designed by Bishop Ranulf (Ralph) Flambard and is particularly noted for its Norman arches. It was still being built in 1113 when monks from Laon in Picardy visited Christchurch. They were on a tour of southern England to raise funds to rebuild Laon Cathedral, which had been destroyed by fire in a riot in which the Bishop of Laon was murdered. The monks brought with them a portable shrine of the Virgin and were outraged when the Dean of Christchurch refused to shelter it.

As the monks sailed from Christchurch, they saw the town consumed by fire. According to Hermann of Laon's dramatic account, a dragon was to blame:

> *But, meanwhile, the just Judge of Heaven did not delay revenge for the slight given to his Mother. We were only about half a league out of town when suddenly two horsemen rode up behind us, shouting out and calling us to come and help the city, which was on fire. We looked back: the whole town had caught fire and was in a blaze. We asked them how it had come to burn and were told that a dragon had come out of the sea and, while we were making our departure, had flown to the city, breathing fire out of its nostrils from which it breathed sulphurous flames. It was flying around from place to place and setting fire to houses one by one.*

Among the houses set ablaze was the Dean's. He escaped aboard ship and returned later; deeply penitent for the vengeance he had brought on Christchurch.

Unfortunately, there is no archaeological or documentary evidence for this blaze in 1113. The Christchurch Antiquarian's website concludes that the "fire" was probably a storm of thunder and lightning, natural phenomena often associated with dragons in medieval accounts.

Left: Detail of the ceiling in Christchurch's beautiful priory.

Following page: The Cross in Hand on Batcombe Hill.

25. Christchurch, Mrs. Perkins's Mausoleum

In the grounds of Christchurch Priory between the church, the castle and the Norman house stands a curious mausoleum erected to the memory of Mrs. Perkins, who died the 1783. She had a horror of being buried alive and requested that her body should not be buried, but placed near what was then the entrance to the free school so that the boys would hear her if she revived. She also requested that the lid of the coffin should not be screwed down and the mausoleum's lock so made that she could open it from the inside. Her wishes were duly carried out, but when her husband died in 1803, her body was removed and the mausoleum re-erected on its present site.

26. The Cross in Hand, Batcombe Hill

A number of legends surround this curious wayside medieval shaft. According to one, a priest from Cerne Abbey was summoned to administer the last rites to a dying shepherd one stormy night. When he reached the stricken man, he realized to his horror that he had lost the little silver box or pyx containing the Holy Sacrament. Unable to perform the last rites without the pyx, he set off at once on the apparently hopeless task of finding it in the dark. All at once, the rain ceased and a shaft of light illuminated the pyx. Gathered about were cattle and wild animals staring in wonder at the miracle. The priest recovered the pyx and returned to the shepherd. In thanksgiving, he later erected the Cross in Hand. The tale is recalled in Thomas Hardy's poem "The Lost Pyx".

Hardy also included the Cross in Hand in *Tess of the D'Urbervilles*, but attaches a much darker legend to it. Alec D'Urberville, the novel's villain, asks Tess to put her hand on top of the stone and swear she will never tempt him with her charms. D'Urberville deceives her in claiming the stone is holy and an old shepherd explains its true origin:

"Cross – no, 'twer not a cross. 'Tis a thing of ill-omen miss. It was put up in wuld times by the relations of a malefactor who was tortured there by nailing his hand to a post, and afterwards hung. The bones lie underneath. They say he sold his soul to the devil, and that he walks at times."

With some imagination, one can see the imprint of a hand on top of the cross. Certainly, it appears to hold some magic power for visitors today, who leave coins as offerings on top. What they hope or wish for is best known to themselves. *(The cross was photographed as found – the author did not place the coins there himself).

Cross in Hand, B3163, 1 mile south-east of Batcombe at ST632037. It stands 250m west of the junction for Batcombe and is guarded by a fence.

27. Pack Monday Fair, Sherborne

"Now is the town alive", wrote a Sherborne resident describing Pack Monday Fair in 1826 (Udal page 131). Held on the Monday after Michaelmas, October 10, Pack Monday Fair may have originated as a hiring fair, such as were traditionally held in country towns each autumn. If so, "pack" may be a corruption of "pact", the agreement between master and servant. Thomas Hardy describes one such hiring fair in *Far From the Madding Crowd*, in the scene where Gabriel Oak offers his services as a shepherd. Alternatively, Pack Fair may refer to packmen, itinerant traders who carried their wares in packs and abounded at country fairs.

Udal (page 130) offers another explanation: "It has been an immemorial custom in Sherborne for the boys to blow horns in the evenings in the streets for some weeks before the fair. It is commonly known as Pack Monday Fair, and there is a tradition that Abbot Peter Ramsam and his workmen completed the nave of the abbey and kept a holiday on that day in 1490, and that the name derived from the men packing up their tools."

Above: The Pack Monday Fair at Sherborne in full swing.
Left: Sherborne Abbey.
Page 33: "Old" Sherborne Castle, the gatehouse.

Traditionally, the fair kicks off when "Teddy Roe's Band" parade through the streets with whistles and tin pans the night before. Teddy Roe was said to have been the Master Mason working on Sherborne Abbey, so the custom is probably ancient, as is the rough music accompanying a "Skimmington Ride" (page 36).

Although it has been revived recently, Teddy Roe's Band was suppressed for some years after anti-social behaviour, which some locals blamed on youths from neighbouring towns. Rowdiness, however, is nothing new: following the rejection of the Great Reform Bill by the House of Lords in 1831, Pack Monday Fair degenerated into three days of rioting.

Lasting all day and well into Monday evening, the fair is now an orderly occasion. It attracts a wide variety of visitors and traders, though some of the entertainments mentioned in the 1826 description quoted above are now missing. These included "the usual merry sights of a country fair – the giant, the learned pig, the giantess and dwarf, the conjuror, the menagerie of wild beasts, the merry-go-round, the lucky bag...".

28. Sherborne's Castles

Michaelmas also sees the return of Sir Walter Raleigh's ghost to Sherborne. However, he comes to visit Sherborne's Old Castle rather than the Pack Fair and his spirit is said to wander the grounds.

One of Elizabethan England's most gifted men, Raleigh excelled as a courtier, poet, explorer, soldier and sailor. A Devonian, he fell in love with Sherborne on his journeys from the court to the West Country and persuaded Queen Elizabeth to grant him the lease on Sherborne Castle. However, he found the medieval castle uninhabitable and started construction on what later became known as New Sherborne Castle in 1594. Raleigh's star, which had risen to such heights earlier in Elizabeth's reign, fell after he aroused the Queen's jealousy by seducing Bessie Throckmorton, one of her maids-of-honour. After a brief imprisonment in the Tower of London, he was released and enjoyed a quieter existence with Bessie (now his wife) in Sherborne. Raleigh's enemies turned Elizabeth's successor, James

I, against him and he was condemned to death in 1603 – although the sentence was not carried out until 1618.

Raleigh was not the first owner of Sherborne Castle to suffer a tragic fall from favour. Edward Seymour, Duke of Somerset, was chief minister to the boy King Edward VI, who was also his nephew. Seymour received Sherborne Castle from his sovereign, in whose name he was effectively ruling England. Such a mighty position was dangerous to hold and Seymour, like Raleigh, was committed to the Tower of London and ended his life on the executioner's block in 1552.

According to legend, these tragedies stem from a curse laid by Osmund, the first Bishop of Salisbury (died 1099) on any secular holder of land belonging to the bishopric of Salisbury. Sherborne Castle was built in the twelfth century by Osmund's successor as Bishop of Salisbury, Roger of Caen (died 1139). After Roger fell out with King Stephen, Sherborne Castle was besieged and taken by the king's forces. The castle's next owners, the Montagues, suffered misfortune, but the curse was lifted once Edward III gave Sherborne back to the Church.

Sherborne Castle became the property of the Crown again under King Henry VIII's sweeping nationalization of Church property. Thus it was passed by Henry VIII's son and heir, Edward, who granted it to the unfortunate Seymour.

Sherborne Castle and grounds, seasonal opening, 01935 812072.
Sherborne Old Castle (English Heritage), seasonal opening, 01935 812730.

Below: "New" Sherborne Castle.

29. Shaftesbury Abbey

King Alfred made Shaftesbury a fortified "burgh", a refuge in case of Viking attack. He then established a Benedictine nunnery at Shaftesbury in 888 and appointed his daughter, Aethelgifu, the first Abbess. Shaftesbury Abbey grew greatly in wealth and importance after King Edward, who had been murdered at Corfe Castle in 978, was buried there (see Corfe Castle page 20). Edward's half-brother and successor, Ethelred the Unready, as well as his step-mother (and supposed murderess), Elfrida endowed the abbey, which drew increasing numbers of pilgrims after Edward was made a saint and martyr in 1001.

Shaftesbury Abbey's prestige was further raised when King Canute came to pray at St Edward's shrine in 1038 and died of a heart attack whilst doing so. Such royal associations made the post of abbess attractive to high born candidates, who often added further to the abbey's wealth from their own store.

With its endowments and regular flow of pilgrims, Shaftesbury Abbey became one of the richest religious houses in the land. It was said that if the Abbot of Glastonbury could have married the Abbess of Shaftesbury they would have held more wealth than the King of England. Indeed, almost everything in the magnificent vista over the Blackmore Vale

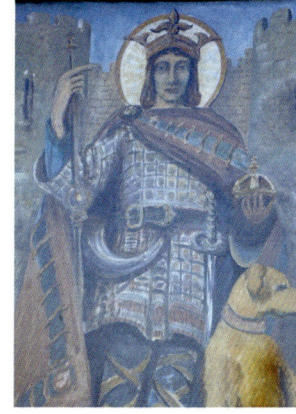

Left: The statue of King Alfred by Andrew Dumont in the garden of Shaftesbury Abbey once stood outside a local middle school.
Below: A painting of King Edward the Martyr in the square at Corfe Castle.

from the abbey once belonged to it – and much more besides.

The considerable size of the abbey church can be gauged by visiting the ruins. These stand in a beautiful and tranquil garden, where medicinal and culinary herbs are grown in the monastic tradition. Visitors enter through an excellent museum and are given an audio guide. This explains the history of Shaftesbury Abbey and the stories behind the various monuments and St Edward's shrine.

Above: All that remains of the abbey are the foundations.

Legend has it that the abbey grounds are haunted by a monk who hid treasure there. Like King Canute, he died suddenly of a heart attack – before he had confided to anyone the location of the treasure. Archaeological excavations have not revealed his treasure, but they have uncovered a wealth of historical artifacts, many of which can be seen in the museum. As well as medieval carvings and tiles, these include the lead casket in which St Edward's bones were found.

Shaftesbury Abbey, SP7 8JR, 01747 852910, seasonal opening. Follow signs from High Street to Park Lane.

30. Skimmington Ride at Montacute House

Montacute House is a splendid sixteenth century mansion just over the border in Somerset. It has many fascinating features, including an extraordinary plaster frieze in the Great Hall depicting a "Skimmington Ride". It was made to tell a story and should be read from left to right.

On the left a woman has caught her errant husband having a crafty drink while he should have been looking after their baby. She beats him over the head with her shoe and this scene is witnessed by a neighbour, who reports it to the community. As a result, the man is paraded through the village mounted on a pole while being forced to play the flute.

According to Udal "Skimmity Riding" is a kind of matrimonial lynch law or pillory intended for those in a lower class of life, who, in certain glaring particulars, may have transgressed their marital duties and have thus brought upon themselves this, the strongest expression of outraged public opinion that a country district is capable of conveying.

Left: A detail from the frieze of the Skimmington Ride in Montacute House.

Below right: The tithe tomb at Thornford Church.

He cites three main reasons for people being subjected to the public humiliation of a Skimmington Ride. The first is when a man and his wife quarrel and he gives up to her. The second is when a woman is unfaithful and her husband submits to the situation and the third case is any grossly licentious conduct on the part of married persons.

The man in the Montacute frieze is treated with contempt because he has submitted to his wife. However, the Skimmington Ride described by Thomas Hardy in *The Mayor of Casterbridge* arises from a mixture of malice, envy and scorn for what Udal called "licentious conduct". Lucetta is so distressed by seeing effigies of herself and Henchard paraded through the streets that she miscarries and consequently dies.

The scene Hardy depicted had ancient roots, but it had not passed into history when he wrote the novel, which was published in 1886. Udal quotes 1884 accounts given in The Bridport News of a Skimmington Ride in Whitchurch Canonicorum and of another Skimmington in Okeford Fitzpaine from The Dorset County Chronicle.

Montacute House (National Trust), TA15 6XP, 01935 823289, ST499172. (Photograph by kind permission of the National Trust.)

31. Thornford Church Tithe Table

Thornford Church's tithe tomb is just outside the south porch on the right. On St Thomas's Day, the vicar sat on this tomb to receive his tithe money, which was paid into a hollow carved out of the top of the tombstone. ST602132.

Calendar of Events

Dorset has a range of annual events. Below is a far from exhaustive selection of some with deep roots in the county's history and customs. All are well established, but depend on public support for their continuance. Times and dates may vary from year to year, those quoted are customary. Please check with the nearest Tourist Information Centre (page 40) before planning a visit. You can also search online for more details. In particular, www.visit-dorset.com has much information about festivals and events in Dorset.

Spring

Shrove Tuesday Football Ceremony, Corfe Castle.
May Fair at Bridport, May Bank Holiday.
Well Dressing at Upwey, May Day.
Morris Dancing at Cerne Abbas Giant, May Day. (page 14)
Abbotsbury Garland Day, May 13.

Summer

Filly Loo Folk Dance Festival, Friday nearest to Midsummer's Day.
Tolpuddle Festival, July. (Page 17)
Gold Hill Fair, Shaftesbury, July.

Autumn

Dorset County Show, Dorchester Showground, early September.
Pack Monday Fair at Sherborne (page 32), Monday after October 10th.

Winter

Mummers Play, Lyme Regis, early January.
Wassailing, various places, January.
Wareham Court Leat, late November.

Knowlton Church inside a Neolithic henge.

Bibliography and Further Reading
Bryant, Arthur, *King Charles II*, Longman, London, 1931.
Osborn, George, *Dorset Curiosities*, Dovecote Press, Dorset, 1986. Accessible miscellany of curious Dorset sites.
Street, Sean, *Tales of Old Dorset*, Countryside Books, 1985. Another helpful miscellany.
Udal, John Symonds, *Dorsetshire Folk-lore*, first published 1922, second edition by Toucan Press, Guernsey, 1970. Still the definitive guide to Dorset's folklore.
Underwood, Peter, *Ghosts of Dorset*, Bossiney Books, Launceston, 2006. Well written account by an acknowledged authority on the paranormal.
Westwood, Robert, *Mysterious Places of Dorset*, Inspiring Places Publishing, Fordingbridge. Companion to this guide.

Websites
www.darkdorset.co.uk A rich trove of informative articles on folklore, customs, legends, ghosts and more.
www.paranormaldatabase.com Rich source of information on the supernatural in Britain.
www.britishlistedbuildings.co.uk Comprehensive factual information on Britain's listed buildings, drawn largely from English Heritage, Cadw and Historic Scotland.
www.mysteriousbritain.co.uk Useful national database.
www.stoneseeker.net Site dedicated to Dorset's ancient mysteries.

Tourist Information Centres

Bournemouth 0845 051 1700
Blandford 01258 454770
Bridport 01308 424901
Christchurch 01202 471780
Dorchester 01305 267992
Lyme Regis 01297 442138
Poole 01202 253253
Portland 01305 861233
Shaftesbury 01747 853514
Sherborne 01935 815341
Swanage 01929 422885
Wareham 01929 552740
Weymouth 01305 785747
Wimborne 01202 886116

"New" Sherborne Castle.